Thorny Scriptures about Women

by Eve Engelbrite

Thorny Scriptures about Women

by Eve Engelbrite

Published by Inspired Idea in the United States of America

©2013, 2016 Eve Engelbrite All rights reserved.

www.InspiredIdeaPress.com

All Scripture quotations are from the American King James Version of the Holy Bible which is in the public domain. It is available for free at www.crosswire.org. Scripture has been *italicized*. **Bold** and <u>underlines</u> have been added to some of the text for emphasis.

ISBN 9781931203326

Contents

	Page
Introduction	vi
God Defined in Genesis	7
Elohim's Image Reflected in Family	9
New Testament definition of Male and Female	12
Adam and Eve's curses and promises were fulfilled	14
Loving Your Husband and Children	16
Headship	27
Silence and Teaching regarding Women	39

BASIC BIBLE STUDY HELPS

All Christians should study the Bible for themselves and allow God's Holy Spirit to guide them into all truth (John 16:13). Don't trust what other people (including me) tell you the Bible says; study it for yourself.

Go to www.e-sword.net and download a free copy of their program containing various Bible versions and concordances and commentaries and maps.

Go to www.crosswire.org/sword/index.jsp and download their free program, and include the American King James Version (AKJV). My husband did an archaic word for modern word substitution of KJV and placed it in the public domain as the American King James Version, which is what I use in my books and studies.

The Hebrew word "selah" in the Psalms is a musical pause or "rest". As a disciple of Jesus Christ, it is a good practice to allow time to digest/ruminate on Scriptures as you read them.

S.T.O.P.P.

SPIRIT - Pray and ask God's Holy Spirit to fill you and guide you into all truth, and give you wisdom.

Thanks - Give thanks for the spiritual food which will nourish your spirit. (like grace before a meal)

Orally recite - Speak the passage out loud to encourage your faith (Romans 10:17).

Pause and **P**onder - which is the meaning of "*Selah*" in Psalms, but can be applied to all Scripture.

Many end their time by writing in a journal what God's Spirit showed them.

For those who want to go deeper . . .

Answer How and the 5 W's (Who, Where, When, What, Why)

Who wrote the passage to whom?

If it is a command, was it specific to that person only, or does it apply to all Jews/Christians?

Where and when was it written?

Did it only apply while the Hebrews were in exile or when a Temple was available?

What is the passage about?

Is it literal, historical, a parable, a prophecy . . .?

Why was it important then, and why is it important now?

Who was effected by it, and does it still have an effect now?

How are you supposed to apply it to your life, if at all?

If it's not applicable, what did you learn from the passage?

If you want to go deeper still, then L.O.O.K.

Look up key words in the concordance for deeper meanings or better translations.

Outline the passage; many patterns emerge by doing so.

Old Testament and New Testament - Is something similar found in both? How are they different?

Know Him - How does it help you know your LORD better? Spend time discussing it with Him.

God Defined in Genesis

> In the beginning **God** created the heaven and the earth.
> And the earth was without form, and void; and
> darkness was on the face of the deep. And the **Spirit** of
> **God** moved on the face of the waters. (Genesis 1:1-2)

> **God** is *elohim* in Hebrew (the suffix "-im" makes the noun
> plural; *elohim* is a masculine plural noun used over 200 times in
> the Bible), meaning more than one god; but as a plural intensive
> noun it has a singular meaning of one God (used over 2,000
> times as such in the Bible).
> **Spirit** is *ruach* in Hebrew (a singular feminine noun), meaning
> breath, mind, and wind; and figuratively life.

God refers to Himself as a complex Being of plurality by using the
word Elohim. His initial act was creating the universe at some
time in the distant past "*in the beginning*". As part of the universe,
the earth was a dark water planet void of life. It is interesting that
the initial biblical introduction to a member of the Godhead refers
to Elohim's Spirit preparing the Earth to sustain life, and that later
Adam names his wife "life/life-giver" (*chavvah* in Hebrew; Eve in
English) based upon life-giving "breath" (*chavah* and *chayah*).

The four sections in this chapter are as follows:

1. Elohim's Image represented as male and female

2. Elohim's Image reflected in the family unit

3. New Testament definitions of male and female

4. Adam and Eve's curses and promises were fulfilled

Elohim's Image represented as Male and Female

The thorny Scriptures about women are in the New Testament.
Paul refers back to Adam and Eve when teaching about women, so
we need to start in Genesis.

The word "feminine" isn't in the Bible. Cultures decide what is
feminine. But the Bible does define being female in relationship to

God and the male. So determine to get the definition of being female from the Bible, not the world.

> And <u>Elohim said, Let us</u> make man in our **image**, after our **likeness**: and let them have dominion over the fish of the sea, and over the fowl of the air, and over the cattle, and over all the earth, and over every creeping thing that creeps on the earth. So Elohim created man in his own image, in the image of Elohim created he him; male and **female** created he them. (Gen. 1:26-27; the word translated "God" in English is replaced with its Hebrew transliteration "Elohim")

> **Image** in Hebrew is *tselem*, meaning phantom or shade, but also mean resemblance or an idol.
> **Likeness** in Hebrew is *demuth*, meaning model, shape, manner or similitude.
> **Dominion** in Hebrew is *radah*, meaning to rule over, to subjugate.
> **Female** in Hebrew is *neqebah* which is also translated woman, from the root word *naqab* meaning to pierce or to bore a hole. The physical purpose of a female is being the sexual counterpart to the male who "pierces" her.

To understand being female we have to understand our Creator. Our word "God" is translated from *Elohim* in this chapter. *Elohim* is a plural noun meaning more than two gods which can be male and/or female (*elohim* is translated "goddess" in I Kings 11:5, 33); yet our God is One.

"Hear, O Israel: The LORD our God is one LORD" (Deut. 6:4) shema yisrael, YHWH Elohim echad YHWH

[Note: in our Bibles when the personal name YHWH (which some pronounce Yahweh and others as Jehovah) occurs, it is translated "LORD" in all capital letters.]

We know the Father and Son were both active in creation (John 1), yet the honor of introduction goes to the Spirit (*ruach*) which is a feminine noun in Genesis 1:2. God's Holy Spirit interacted personally with our planet, fluttering or vibrating (*rachaph*) over the waters like a hen brooding over her chicks.

After our planet was terraformed with appropriate light sources and flora and fauna, the Father, Son and Spirit created humans in a male and female form in accordance to their Image as male and female; the Father and Son are both male, so that leaves the female aspect to the Spirit.

Eve was formed from Adam's flesh and bone which represented the "one flesh" oneness of the man and woman before they had intercourse. The Oneness of Elohim is nonsexual. The male and female humans were both given dominion over the creatures of the earth, similar to Elohim having dominion over the universe. They were both commanded to be fruitful and multiply and fill the Earth.

Let the Holy Spirit (*ruach hakodesh*) plant those seeds of truth deep into your spirit.

[Pause and discuss it with your LORD.]

Elohim's Image reflected in the family

I'm not a feminist; I don't refer to Elohim as she, but Biblically we should refer to the Holy Spirit as She instead of He or It in the Old Testament. Elohim is a complete family unit: Father, Spirit, and Son. Elohim did not give the angels the ability to reproduce, but He gave reproduction abilities to the animals and humans. Part of being created in Elohim's Image is the ability to make a family unit, which He made very clear in Genesis chapter 2.

> And the LORD God said, It is not good that the man should be **alone**; I will make him an **help meet** for him. . . . And the LORD God caused a deep sleep to fall on Adam, and he slept: and he took one of his ribs, and closed up the flesh instead thereof; And the **rib**, which the LORD God had taken from man, made he a woman, and brought her to the man. And Adam said, This is now bone of my bones, and flesh of my flesh: she shall be called **Woman**, because she was taken out of **Man**. Therefore shall a man leave his father and his mother, and shall join to his wife: and they shall be one flesh. (Gen. 2:18, 21-24)

> **Alone** in Hebrew is *bad*, meaning separate or apart.
> **Help** in Hebrew is *ezer* meaning succour from the root word meaning "to surround".
> **Meet** in Hebrew is *neged* meaning suitable from the root word *nagad* meaning facing boldly opposite.
> **Rib** in Hebrew is *tsela* meaning curved or side (appendage, some say a baculum), and only translated as rib in this Scripture.
> **Man** is *ish*, and **woman** is *ishshah*.

Even though Adam had a perfect relationship with Elohim, he needed a counterpart (*neged*) to mate with (which he noticed after naming all the animal pairs). Adam especially needed a helper (*ezer*); "succour" means to assist during times of need and literally to run to give aid, or to go beneath (in order to lift the other up). Elohim is referred to as our Help in Psalms 33:20, 70:5, 115:9-11 and 124:8. Truly the female was created in the Image and Likeness of God, just as the male was. I believe they were also both initially immortal like God.

God created man from the soil; and Adam tended the garden, and would work the soil for sustenance. God created woman from man's *tsela* ("rib" or baculum, a penis bone, according to Dundes and Zevit); and Eve would be Adam's wife and the mother of all living, emphasizing her reproductive organs. Man and woman were created according to their purpose.

Elohim was very clear that before man and woman sexually joined, the man was to leave his parents in order to establish a new family unit with his wife; and the husband and wife would become a new single unit of "one flesh" much like Elohim is one family unit of "One Spirit" yet separate individuals.

The sexual union of husband and wife would also represent the Oneness of Christ with His Bride, the Church (Eph. 5:31-32) in answer to His prayer in John 17:21-23. Elohim created male and female in His Image so that in their sexual union they would experience the intimacy and joy of oneness and eventually conceive a child which would bring another aspect of joy and wonder into their lives. Elohim expressed Himself in creating a family so that all humans could relate to their Creator: Father, Spirit, and Son.

So male, female, marriage and family are the foci of Satan's attacks in order to distort the human concept of Elohim; and we spend most of our Christian lives healing from the distortion and damage.

[Pause and ask God's Holy Spirit to heal your concepts of male, female, marriage and family.]

Heathen Heavenly Family Units

Egypt

Egypt was possibly the earliest empire on earth. Their creation myths parallel Genesis in several ways. They combined the creator and the first man, which they call Atum.

> Atum was a self-created deity, the first being to emerge from the **darkness** and <u>endless watery abyss</u> that girdled the world before creation. A product of the energy and matter contained in this chaos, he created divine and human beings through loneliness: <u>alone</u> in the universe, he produced from his own <u>sneeze,</u> or in some accounts, semen, Shu, the god of air, and Tefnut, the goddess of moisture. The <u>brother and sister</u>, and husband and wife . . . – Wikipedia

Atum's wife was Iusaset who is described as the "grandmother of all of the deities". She is also associated with the acacia tree which was viewed as the "tree of life". Some taught that Atum and Iusaset gave birth to Shu and Tefnut, and since there were no others; brothers and sisters had to marry each other (a tradition Egypt's pharaohs continued and reaped the genetic consequences).

Sumeria to Saudi Arabia

Nimrod established his kingdom in the land of Shinar which scholars call Sumer. The Sumerians were a very early civilization which used cuneiform writing from its beginning. They have recovered many tablets of their myths and legends which sound very similar to the first chapters of Genesis, like the *Epic of Gilgamesh* which parallels Noah's ark.

The Sumerian chief gods were Enlil and Ninlil who gave birth to a son named Nanna. Nanna was the moon god called Sin by the Akkadians who built major temples to him in Haran, Jericho, and throughout the Arabian and Sinai peninsulas. The desert of Sin is in the *Sin*ai. Nanna was later called Allah, "the deity," by Mohammed. Nanna had three daughters which were later worshipped in Mecca and named in the "Satanic verses" of Koran (Sura 53:19-20).

Nanna and his wife Ningal gave birth to a daughter named Inanna, the "queen of heaven" who was known as Ishtar to the Akkadians. Other myths place Inanna as the daughter of the Sumerian creator god, An. Inanna/Ishtar was the sex goddess who had many temples of prostitution built for her.

Ishtar's lover was named Tammuz, the shepherd god. Ishtar braved the underworld after the death of Tammuz and somehow resurrected him and herself. Each summer solstice the death of Tammuz was mourned for six days (even in Israel, Ezekiel 8:14-15), and a summer month was named after him. Tammuz was later called Adonis by the Greeks, and he represented a false Christ, just as his immortal parents represented a false king and queen of heaven.

The early religions mimicked the truth of the Oneness of Elohim as a family unit. Elohim makes it clear we are to worship the LORD as One Being, not as three separate gods.

NT definitions of male and female

> And he [Jesus] answered and said to them, Have you not read, that he which made them at the beginning made them **male** and **female** . . . (Matthew 19:4)

Male in Greek is *arsen;* possibly from the word *airo* meaning to lift.
Female in Greek is *thelus;* root *thele* meaning nipple and the word *thelazo* meaning to suckle.

The OT definition of female focussed on her being a sexual counterpart; the NT definition of female emphasized the ability to breast feed and raise children. Paul used these same terms in the following:

> For as many of you as have been baptized into Christ
> have put on Christ. There is neither Jew nor Greek,
> there is neither bond nor free, there is neither **male** nor
> **female**: for you are all one in Christ Jesus.
> (Galatians 3:27-28)

Note that the purpose of Christ's church was to emulate Elohim's Oneness. Society categorizes people according to their ethnicity, social status, and sex; but all those baptized into Christ are a "new creation" exemplifying His Oneness.

The early church had to root out their prejudices between Jews and Greeks (Acts 6:1-6), between rich and poor (James 2:1-9), and between male and female.

During the 70 years of captivity in Babylon (606-536 BC), the Jews compiled copies of the Law, the Prophets, and the other Writings, which they refer to as the *Tanakh*, and we call the Old Testament. They also wrote commentaries on the Tanakh mixed with legends and their **traditions** which is called the *Talmud*. These traditions were an unnecessary and burdensome yoke upon the people. Regarding women the Babylonian Talmud stated women were possessions of men, women could not be witnesses in a court of law, and a woman's voice was not to be heard in public.

Jesus came to negate the authority of Jewish "traditions" and restore sole authority to the Word of God. Jesus liberated women and restored their God-given honor.

> Then the Pharisees and scribes asked him, Why walk
> not your disciples according to the **tradition** of the
> elders, but eat bread with unwashed hands? He
> answered and said to them, Well has Esaias prophesied
> of you hypocrites, as it is written, This people honors
> me with their lips, but their heart is far from me.
> However, in vain do they worship me, teaching for
> doctrines **the commandments of men**. For laying

> aside the commandment of God, you hold the
> **tradition** of men, as the washing of pots and cups: and
> many other such like things you do. And he said to
> them, Full well <u>you reject the commandment of God,
> that you may keep your own</u> **tradition**. (Mark 7:5-9)

Tradition in Greek is *paradosis* meaning oral law.

Beware lest any man spoil you through philosophy and vain deceit, after the **tradition** of men, after the rudiments of the world, and not after Christ. (Colossians 2:8)

The Bible honors your importance as a female created in God's Image, even if the traditions of your culture do not.

Adam and Eve's curses and promises were fulfilled

According to the chronology of Geneses 2:16-20, God commanded Adam not to eat of the tree of knowledge of good and evil before the woman was created. Adam may have added "neither touch it" when he told Eve God's command, or she may have added it herself as an extra barrier; but adding to God's Word is never right (Proverbs 30:5-6).

Deception and Curses

> For Adam was first formed, then Eve. And Adam was
> not deceived, but the woman being **deceived** was in the
> transgression. (I Timothy 2:13-14)

Deceived is *apatao* in Greek, meaning cheated, deluded, and beguiled.

Eve was tricked into eating the fruit; whereas Adam disobeyed with full understanding of what he was doing. Eve justified her actions as we do today (I John 2:16), and ate the fruit and gave it to Adam who was "with" (*'im*, meaning equally with) her, and both knew they were naked (Gen. 3:7). Pre-incarnate Christ walked in the garden and heard Adam blame Eve, and then Eve blamed the serpent who "beguiled" (*nasha*, meaning deceive, delude, or seduce); and then God gave a curse and promise to the serpent, to Eve, and to Adam. The curses are specific to the individual and not general: Eve was cursed, not all women; Adam was cursed, not all men. [The curse is separated from the promise below.]

> To the woman he said, I will greatly multiply your
> **sorrow** and your **conception**; in **sorrow** you shall
> **bring forth** children;
> and your **desire** shall be to your husband, and he shall
> **rule** over you. (Gen. 3:16)

> **Sorrow** is *'itstsabone*, meaning worrisomeness, from a bad
> sense of fashioning (like twisting a paper out of anxiety).
> **Conception** is *herayon*, meaning pregnancy.
> **Sorrow** is *'etseb*, meaning painful toil and labor.
> **Bring forth** is *yalad*, meaning begit or travail.
> **Desire** is *teshuqah*, meaning to flow towards; also used in
> "I am my beloved's, and his desire is toward me." (Song
> 7:10), from *shuq* meaning to overflow or to give abundance
> **Rule** is *mashal*, meaning to have power or dominion.

Eve's curse was painful labor and worry during pregnancy. Adam lived to be 930 years and had many sons and daughters (Gen. 5:4-5); therefore Eve likely had several hundred painful pregnancies. My understanding is God's promise to Eve was that she would overflow with love for Adam, and Adam would have authority over her to protect her so she needn't fear ever leading them into sin again. The promise of her husband ruling over her was specifically to Eve, not all women. The curse of pain in childbirth was not for all women but specifically to Eve. Some women have rather painless natural births.

> And to Adam he said, Because you have listened to the
> voice of your wife, and have eaten of the tree, of which
> I commanded you, saying, You shall not eat of it:
> cursed is the ground for your sake; in sorrow shall you
> eat of it all the days of your life; Thorns also and

> thistles shall it bring forth to you; and you shall eat the
> herb of the field;
> In the sweat of your face shall you eat bread, till you
> return to the ground; for out of it were you taken: for
> dust you are, and to dust shall you return.
> (Genesis 3:17-19)

Husbands listening to their wives is a good thing unless the wife is convincing you to sin. God cursed the ground which produced the fruit that they had eaten, and now it would produce painful thorns and thistles during Adam's now mortal life. And that was the good news, Adam wasn't going to live forever in his sinful state. The Bible does not say if Adam and Eve repented, but I hope they did.

The curse on Adam's "ground" (*erets Adam*) ceased hundreds of years before Noah's flood. But the escalating violence evoked another curse which would destroy that supercontinent. (The myth of a highly technological world destroyed by flood was possibly "*Adam erets*" degrading over millennia to "Atlantis".)

[Pause. If you have believed Eve's curse applied to you, renounce it. We are not to live under curses, but empowered by the promises of God in Christ (Gal. 3:8-18)]

The Promised Seed

The promise which was yet to be fulfilled in the future was the one Elohim gave to the serpent:

> And I will put enmity between you and the woman,
> and between your seed and her seed; it shall bruise
> your head, and you shall bruise his heel. (Gen. 3:15)

Elohim reiterated the promise of the redeeming Seed to Abraham (Gen.12:7).

> Now to Abraham and his seed were the promises made.
> He said not, And to seeds, as of many; but as of one,
> And to your **seed**, which is Christ. And this I say, that
> the covenant, that was confirmed before of God in
> Christ, the law, which was four hundred and thirty

years after, cannot cancel, that it should make the promise of none effect. For if the inheritance be of the law, it is no more of promise: but God gave it to Abraham by promise. Why then serves the law? It was added because of transgressions, till the seed should come to whom the promise was made; and it was ordained by angels in the hand of a mediator. Now a mediator is not a mediator of one, but God is one. (Gal. 3:16-20)

Which brings us back to why Elohim created humans as male and female: to portray His Oneness.

Loving Your Husband and Children

Loving your husband and children is divided into the following four parts:

1. Connect the creation and union of Adam and Eve to Christ and His Bride.

2. Love your husband by respecting him and giving him honor and "reverence".

3. Love your husband by having sex more often with him.

4. Love your children.

Connect the creation and union of Adam and Eve to Christ and His Bride.

Elohim created male and female in His Image (Gen. 1:26-31), but chose to create Eve out of Adam's side, so that even before they had sex, Adam recognized Eve as part of himself (Gen. 2:20-24). Paul wrote that Adam was a "figure" of Christ (Romans 5:14), and he called Christ the "last Adam" (I Cor. 15:45). Though not written, I think Paul is alluding to Christ's Bride figuratively being taken from Christ's side where He was pierced and the blood and water flowed out (John 19:34) providing our redemption and adoption into His family.

For we are members of his body, of his flesh, and of his bones. For this cause shall a man leave his father and mother, and shall be joined to his wife, and they two shall be one flesh. This is a great mystery: but I speak concerning Christ and the church. Nevertheless let every one of you in particular <u>so love his wife even as himself; and the wife see that she reverence her husband</u>. (Ephesians 5:30-33)

Reverence is *phobeo* in Greek from *phobos* (fear, dread, terror), meaning to be afraid; and by analogy to be in awe of, to reverence, to venerate, or to treat with deference or reverential obedience.

Because of the sacrificial love of Christ, the Bride is to reverence and obey the Lord. Paul encourages husbands to see their wives as an extension of their own bodies, and to have the same sacrificial love for their wives that Christ has for His Church. Using the same analogy, the wife is to reverence her husband. The commands to husbands and wives are not conditional; Paul didn't write "if" your husband loves you sacrificially, then reverence him.

God saw it was not good for man to be alone (Gen. 2:18), even though he had a perfect relationship with God. He created a woman to meet the needs which He could not. It is a high honor to be a wife.

Love your husband by respecting him and giving him honor and "reverence".

Women need to feel loved and protected, but men need to feel respected and reverenced (feared). Love and respect are the engine of the marriage which either spouse can rev up.

Modern definitions (from dictionary.com) regarding reverence (*phobeo*):

A. Reverence is "a feeling or attitude of deep respect tinged with awe."

B. Venerate is "to hold in deep respect, to honour <u>in recognition of</u>

qualities; or to solicit the good will of."

C. Deference is the "respectful submission or yielding to the judgment, opinion, or will of another; or respectful or courteous regard by deferring to another."

D. Obedience can be the "recognition of another's sphere of authority by dutiful or submissive compliance."

I am not suggesting a wife should be a doormat or stay in an abusive relationship. I am saying that a wife's reverence of her husband should reflect the reverence the church gives to Jesus Christ. None of us are perfect, but wives can choose to have an attitude of respect toward their husbands (A). Wives can recognize the good qualities in their husbands and speak of them privately and publicly (B). Wives can defer to their husband's opinion or judgment in a matter (C) and not say "I told you so" if it doesn't work out. Wives can recognize their husband's authority as head of the household, and dutifully comply to requests without contempt or complaining (D). Wives can be less selfish and think of ways to bless their husbands (B).

> There is difference also between a wife and a virgin.
> The unmarried woman cares for the things of the Lord,
> that she may be holy both in body and in spirit: but she
> that is married cares for the things of the world, how
> she may please her husband. (I Cor. 7:34)

[Though remaining unmarried allows a woman to devote herself completely to the Lord and His work, celibacy is not a more admirable state than marriage. The Catholic church forbidding people to marry in order to serve God is a sin (I Timothy 4:1-3).]

"Marriage is honorable in all, and the bed undefiled: but fornicators and adulterers God will judge." (Hebrews 13:4)]

Honoring Your Marriage Vows

The traditional marriage vows are the commitment of the husband and wife to love each other and stay united through sickness, financial troubles, and various hard times. Peter and I wrote our own vows, and each anniversary we reconfirm them as we read them to each other; 25 times so far.

>Peter: "I cried to God for a wife to love and to cherish, and today He has answered my cry."

Your marriage is an act of God's will together with an act of your will.

Cherish: you need a "giving" love, not a "taking" love.

> Whoever finds a wife finds a good thing, and obtains favor of the LORD. (Pr. 18:22)

>Eve: "I desired a godly husband, and God has given me you."

Remember to thank God for the GIFT He has given you in your spouse. Like salvation, you didn't work to deserve him, and works won't keep him; it's a love commitment.

> Every good gift and every perfect gift is from above,
> and comes down from the Father of lights, with whom
> is no fickleness, neither shadow of turning.
> (James 1:17)

>Peter: "I will love you as Christ loved the church and gave Himself up for her."

This is the basis for the husband's authority in the home, not his ability to get her to submit.

> Husbands, love your wives, even as Christ also loved
> the church, and gave himself for it; That he might
> sanctify and cleanse it with the washing of water by the
> word (Eph. 5:25-26)

>Eve: "I trust you, and I will honor you and submit myself to you."

This is God's way for wives to be fulfilled in marriage. (Gen. 3:16)

> Wives, submit yourselves to your own husbands, as to
> the Lord. For the husband is the head of the wife, even
> as Christ is the head of the church: (Eph. 5:22-23)

>Peter: "I will keep my heart open to the needs of your heart."

Your wife's problem is your problem; "our" problem to work through together.

> So ought men to love their wives as their own bodies.
> He that loves his wife loves himself. For no man ever
> yet hated his own flesh; but nourishes and cherishes it,
> even as the Lord the church: (Eph. 5:28-29)

>Eve: "I will keep my heart open to you and seek your good."

Don't build walls, build bridges; your delay could bring about harm.

> I sleep, but my heart wakes: it is the voice of my beloved
> that knocks, saying, Open to me, my sister, my love, my
> dove, my undefiled: for my head is filled with dew, and my
> locks with the drops of the night. I have put off my coat;
> how shall I put it on? I have washed my feet; how shall I
> defile them? My beloved put in his hand by the hole of the
> door, and my bowels were moved for him. I rose up to open
> to my beloved; and my hands dropped with myrrh, and my
> fingers with sweet smelling myrrh, on the handles of the
> lock. I opened to my beloved; but my beloved had
> withdrawn himself, and was gone: my soul failed when he
> spoke: I sought him, but I could not find him; I called him,
> but he gave me no answer. The watchmen that went about
> the city found me, they smote me, they wounded me; the
> keepers of the walls took away my veil from me. I charge
> you, O daughters of Jerusalem, if you find my beloved, that
> you tell him, that I am sick of love. (Song 5:2-8)

>Peter: "I accept you, and I will encourage your growth."

You accept your wife as she is, but don't try to keep her there.

Expectations and conditions are incompatible with acceptance.

> Why receive you one another, as Christ also received
> us to the glory of God. (Rom. 15:7)

>Eve: "I accept you, and I will encourage your growth."

The world continually yells at us, "You are unacceptable," so counter it by constantly affirming your love and acceptance of your mate.

> Let no corrupt communication proceed out of your mouth, but that which is good to the use of edifying, that it may minister grace to the hearers. (Eph. 4:29)

>Peter: "I will be a protector and lover to you."

It's your job to take the brunt of the world. Don't neglect HER sexual needs.

> Likewise, you husbands, dwell with them according to knowledge, giving honor to the wife, as to the weaker vessel, and as being heirs together of the grace of life; that your prayers be not hindered. (I Peter 3:7)

> Let the husband render to the wife due benevolence: and likewise also the wife to the husband. The wife has not power of her own body, but the husband: and likewise also the husband has not power of his own body, but the wife. (I Corinthians 7:3-4)

>Eve: "I will be a helper and lover to you."

Choose to be a part of your husband's work.

> Two are better than one; because they have a good reward for their labor. (Ecclesiastes. 2:9)

Life-long lovers have a "you, and no other" mind-set.

> Marriage is honorable in all, and the bed undefiled: but fornicators and adulterers God will judge. (Hebrews 13:4)

>Peter: "I will never leave you nor forsake you." (Heb. 13:5)

Love is a commitment.

> But from the beginning of the creation God made them male and female. For this cause shall a man leave his father and mother, and join to his wife; And they two

shall be one flesh: so then they are no more two, but one flesh. What therefore God has joined together, let not man put asunder. (Mark 10:6-9)

>Eve: "I will support you and stand with you always."

Whether he's right or wrong, choose to stick it out TOGETHER.

Likewise, you wives, be in subjection to your own husbands; that, if any obey not the word, they also may without the word be won by the conversation of the wives; While they behold your chaste conversation coupled with fear. Whose adorning let it not be that outward adorning of plaiting the hair, and of wearing of gold, or of putting on of apparel; But let it be the hidden man of the heart, in that which is not corruptible, even the ornament of a meek and quiet spirit, which is in the sight of God of great price. For after this manner in the old time the holy women also, who trusted in God, adorned themselves, being in subjection to their own husbands: Even as Sara obeyed Abraham, calling him lord: whose daughters you are, as long as you do well, and are not afraid with any amazement. (I Peter 3:1-6)

For a comprehensive study on the life of Sarah as it relates to being a woman of God, go to my free on-line book at http://engelbrite.com/inspiredidea/ans2abuse/WOMANGOD.html

Additional tips:

As a wife your primary service is to your husband (I Cor. 7:34), and it is the greatest testimony of your relationship to Jesus. We have the privilege of demonstrating before the world how the church serves Jesus by serving and submitting to our husbands.

Refuse to depend on yourself alone for the "right" answers. Choose to relate to God and your husband in decision making. Don't make your own decision separately and then bring it before God or your husband for approval/disapproval; instead choose to make the decision with God and your husband TOGETHER.

Before you can be open, you need to trust. Before you can trust, you need to believe your acceptance is not based upon your works but is a gracious commitment. If you are fearful, recall your husband's loving acts toward you. Then remember your problem is OUR problem, and ask, "What's best for US?"

The world's ideas of success are based upon I John 2:16; the lust of the flesh (materialism, sex, food and drink), the lust of the eyes (appearance, clothes, car, jewelry), and the boastful pride of life (corporate ladder, finanaces, power). Don't badger your spouse to become more successful in order to provide more things; be content and thankful with what you have. Don't criticize your mate's appearance.

Love your husband by having sex more often with him.

God created humans as sexual beings. His command to Adam and Eve to be fruitful and multiply (Gen. 1:28) was never rescinded, but was reestablished after Noah's flood (Gen. 8:17).

> Let the husband render to the wife due benevolence: and likewise also the wife to the husband. The wife has not power of her own body, but the husband: and likewise also the husband has not power of his own body, but the wife. Defraud you not one the other, except it be with consent for a time, that you may give yourselves to fasting and prayer; and come together again, that Satan tempt you not for your incontinency. (I Cor. 7:3-5)

Defraud is *apostereo* in Greek meaning to deprive, hold back, despoil, or rob.
Consent is *sumphonos* in Greek meaning mutual or harmonious agreement.
Incontinency is *akrasia* in Greek meaning lack of self-control.

Conjugal rights are the sexual rights and privileges conferred on spouses by the marriage contract. Marital acts should not be physically painful nor emotionally demeaning to either spouse; nor should they include sin (like forcing a spouse to watch porn or to have sex with someone else). Sex should never be withheld unless both spouses agree to do so in order to consecrate themselves to a couple days of prayer. Don't use sex to manipulate your spouse. If one spouse is sick or injured, together they should find a way to still have times of intimacy.

In Bible times, the father of the bride would arrange a bride-price the bridegroom would have to pay (Gen. 29:15-30), and the wife would be required to provide sex on command. But in the above Scripture Paul shows the equality of mutual ownership of husband and wife. Neither spouse should have to demand sex if the husband is loving his wife and the wife is honoring her husband. There's nothing wrong with sitting down with a calendar and your schedules and planning some of your sexual engagements. You also might want to have a special word of phrase which will let your spouse know you would really like to have sex now.

Newlyweds should not overextend themselves their first year, but stick close to home.

> When a man has taken a new wife, he shall not go out
> to war, neither shall he be charged with any business:
> but he shall be free at home one year, and shall cheer
> up his wife which he has taken. (Deuteronomy 24:5)

Love your children.

The man and woman of faith in Christ have blessed children and are blessed by their children.

> The just man walks in his integrity: his children are
> blessed after him. (Proverbs 20:7)

> Her children arise up, and call her blessed; her husband
> also, and he praises her. (Proverbs 31:28)

So primarily, love your children by living out your faith in Christ honestly before them, and by giving them the opportunity to grow in their faith in Christ.

> The aged women likewise, that they be in behavior as
> becomes holiness, not false accusers, not given to
> much wine, teachers of good things; That they may
> teach the young women to be sober, to love their
> husbands, to love their children, To be discreet, chaste,
> keepers at home, good, obedient to their own husbands,
> that the word of God be not blasphemed. (Titus 2:3-5)

Teach to be Sober is *sophronizo* in Greek meaning to make of
sound mind, to discipline toward self-control.
Love their Husbands is *philandros* in Greek literally meaning
to love men, but specifically to be affectionate toward your
husband. Similar to Philadelphia, which means to love brothers.
Love their Children is *philoteknos* in Greek, meaning to love
children.
Discreet is *sophron* in Greek meaning to be self-controlled or
moderate in behavior.
Chaste is *hagnos* in Greek meaning clean, innocent, modest, and
pure.
Keepers at home is *oikouros* in Greek (*oikos* is home and *ouros*
is guard) meaning home guard.
Good is *agathos* in Greek meaning to be of benefit.
Obedient is *hupotasso* in Greek, literally meaning under
obedience to, or orderly as arranged.

Sober actions and thoughts bring about much peace. It's hard
taking our thoughts captive to Christ (II Cor. 10:5) when single,
but it's even more important when we're married. Do your best to
think well of your husband, and to avoid blaming him. Be careful
not to belittle your husband or children through sarcasm.

Though there is a sexual attraction, your husband also needs your
love as his friend and confidant who would never betray his trust
by gossiping about him. Demonstrate respect for your husband's
and children's privacy and self-esteem by not sharing their
shortcomings with others unless it's something you agree together
can be shared without harm.

Most parents demonstrate love to their children by giving them
good gifts (Matthew 7:11; James 1:17). What's harder is to
lovingly and consistently discipline your children (Heb.12:5-11).

In order to teach them self-control, you have to demonstrate self-control. If you want your children to remain pure and innocent, you have to guard the home from evil influences. That means only allowing godly books, music, videos, TV, and games into your home, and placing parental locks on electronic devices. What's acceptable for a 13 year old to view will not usually be acceptable for a 3 year old; and so you train older children to help you guard what their younger siblings do and see. You might also want to consider homeschooling or placing your children in Christian schools.

> Hear, O Israel: The LORD our God is one LORD: And you shall love the LORD your God with all your heart, and with all your soul, and with all your might. And these words, which I command you this day, shall be in your heart: And you shall teach them diligently to your children, and shall talk of them when you sit in your house, and when you walk by the way, and when you lie down, and when you rise up. And you shall bind them for a sign on your hand, and they shall be as frontlets between your eyes. And you shall write them on the posts of your house, and on your gates. (Deuteronomy 6:4-9)

It's fine to be strict with your children as long as you are also being good-natured and loving toward them. Any household rules are not to empower you but to provide safety for them. You and your husband need to sit down together to compose your household rules, and to present them to the children together as rules you will both enforce. If something new comes along, and you and your husband view it differently, discuss it in private and come to an agreement; don't debate the issue in front of your kids. The same applies for marital problems; don't have arguments in front of your kids or use the kids as pawns in your battle.

As you demonstrate your love and respect for your husband as he continues to grow in Christ, your children are more likely to feel safe and accepted as they mature.

Headship

The four sections of headship are as follows:

1. Honor biblical headship, but not man's traditions.

2. Submit yourself to your husband because it represents the Bride submitting to Christ.

3. (*Hupotasso*) Obey and subject yourself to your husband.

4. Christ will subdue (*hupotasso*) all things unto His Father, including Himself.

Honor Biblical Headship, but not Man's Traditions

Father, mother, child; a progression of headship in the family which began in Genesis.

The holy Father sent His Son to Earth and commanded the Son what to do and say (John 12:49).

Messiah, the Son of God, obeyed the Father, and the Father exalted the Son (Phil. 2:8-11).

Even though Jesus and the Father are One, there is submission within that Oneness.

As a child, Jesus submitted to His earthly parents. During His ministry, Jesus' mother submitted herself to Him as Messiah, and placed her trust in His redemption as all His disciples did in order to become a member of the family of God (Matthew 12:46-50; Acts 1:14). All of Christ's disciples received His Spirit after Messiah returned to the Father's side in heaven.

> Nevertheless I tell you the truth; It is expedient for you that I go away: for if I go not away, the **Comforter** will not come to you; but if I depart, I will send him to you. And when he is come, he will reprove the world of sin, and of righteousness, and of judgment: Of sin, because they believe not on me; Of righteousness, because I go to my Father, and you see me no more; Of judgment, because the prince of this world is judged. I have yet

many things to say to you, but you cannot bear them
now. However, when he, the **Spirit** of truth, is come,
he will guide you into all truth: for <u>he shall not speak
of himself</u>; but whatever he shall hear, that shall he
speak: and he will show you things to come. <u>He shall
glorify me</u>: for he shall receive of mine, and shall show
it to you. <u>All things that the Father has are mine:
therefore said I, that he shall take of mine, and shall
show it to you</u>. (John 16:7-15)

Comforter in Greek is *parakletos*, a masculine noun meaning
called to one's side to help or succour.
Comfort in Greek is *paraklesis*, a feminine noun, is used as
"comfort in the Holy Spirit" (Acts 9:31) and as *"comfort of the
Scriptures"* (Romans 15:4).
Spirit in Greek is *pneuma*, a neuter noun from the root word
pneo meaning to breathe or to blow.

As Christians we interact with the Holy Spirit everyday, but we
rarely praise the Holy Spirit as an individual because the function
of "Comforter" and "Spirit of truth" is to proclaim the words of the
Son of God and glorify the Messiah. The Son possesses what the
Father has, and the Spirit takes of the Son and reveals it to us.
Because *pneuma* is neuter, the Holy Spirit is often referred to as
"It" in the New Testament.

Likewise the Spirit also helps our infirmities: for we
know not what we should pray for as we ought: but the
Spirit itself makes intercession for us with groanings
which cannot be uttered. And he that searches the
hearts knows what is the mind of the Spirit, because he
makes intercession for the saints according to the will
of God. (Romans 8:26-27)

Helps is *sunantilambanomai* meaning "to lay hold along with,"
to help/strive to obtain with others; or to take hold with another.
Infirmities is *astheneia* meaning weakness, disease, or sickness.
Groanings is *stenagmos* meaning a groaning or a sigh.
Cannot be uttered is *alaletos* meaning "not spoken" or not
expressed in words.

It's a great comfort to know while we are writhing in pain, or groaning with grief, or sighing from despair, or silenced by fear; that God's Holy Spirit is holding us and helping us through it while supplicating the Father on our behalf.

[Pause, and receive the comfort of God's Holy Spirit, and ask for help in submission.]

How headship effects the family and church

Christ bought His Bride with His own blood ("you are bought with a price," I Cor. 6:20); Jesus owns us and He is our Lord and we are obligated to obey Him. We are not obligated to obey the "traditions of men" (Mark 7:8-9).

The Mishnah is Jewish oral traditions which were written down 200 years after Christ. The Mishnah gives the following behaviors as grounds for divorce: "appearing in public with loose hair, weaving in the marketplace, and talking to any man" as violations of *Dat Yehudit*, which means Jewish rule, as opposed to *Dat Moshe*, meaning Mosaic rule. Thus covering of the hair by a married woman was a modesty standard defined by the Jewish community. Orthodox women still shave their heads when they marry and wear a wig instead so that their husbands can not divorce them for displaying a "loose hair in public". Also a hair covering clearly showed a woman was married, much as wedding rings do today.

The tradition of Jewish men covering their heads with a skullcap or a prayer shawl (*tallit*) may have occurred during the Babylonian exile. In the East, to show respect, men covered their heads; but in the West, men remove their head covering to show respect.

The married Jewish women of Paul's day wore head-scarves; the Greek married women wore a yellow head-scarf. Corinth is located in Greece. Though the Corinthian Christians were free in Christ from this tradition, the Christian married women continued to wear head-scarves in order to honor their husbands, even though their own hair was covering enough before the Lord.

Among Jews, Greeks, and Romans, adulteresses sometimes had their hair cropped as a humiliating punishment for their crime.

Among the Jews this was done as someone recited the words, "because thou hast departed from the manner of the daughters of Israel, who go with their head covered … therefore that has befallen thee which thou hast chosen." [Alfred Edersheim, *Sketches of Jewish Social Life in the Days of Christ* (London: Religious Tract Society, 1876), p. 154.]

Now I praise you, brothers, that you remember me in all things, and keep the **ordinances**, as I delivered them to you. **But** I would have you know, that the **head** of **every man** is Christ; and the head of [the] **woman** is the man; and the head of Christ is God.
<u>Every man</u> praying or prophesying, having his head covered, dishonors his head. But <u>every woman</u> that **prays** or **prophesies** with her head uncovered dishonors her head: for that is even all one as if she were shaven.
For if **the** <u>woman</u> be not covered, let her also be shorn: but if it be a shame for a woman to be shorn or shaven, let her be covered. For a man indeed ought not to cover his head, for as much as he is the image and glory of God: but the woman is the glory of the man.
For [the] man is not of [the] woman: but [the] woman of [the] man. Neither was [the] man created for the woman; but the woman for the man. For this cause ought the woman to have **power** on her head because of the **angels**. Nevertheless neither is [the] man without [the] woman, neither [the] woman without [the] man, in the Lord. For as the woman is of the man, even so is the man also by the woman; but all things of God. Judge in yourselves: is it comely that a woman pray to God uncovered? Does not even nature itself teach you, that, if a man have long hair, it is a shame to him? But if a woman have long hair, it is a glory to her: for her hair is given her for a covering. But if any man seem to be contentious, we have no such **custom**, neither the churches of God. (I Cor. 11:2-16; words in brackets were added by translator and aren't in the Greek text)

Ordinances in Greek is *paradosis* literally meaning "giving over" as oral teaching; and the dozen other times it is translated as "tradition(s)".

Custom in Greek is *sunetheia* literally meaning "with manners". Used one other place in John 18:39.

But in Greek is *de*, and can also be translated "and" or "now".

Head in Greek is *kaphale*, a feminine noun, always translated "head(s)", and can also mean source or origin; but metaphorically means chief or prominent. It's based on the word *kapto*, meaning seizing; as in seizing power.

Every in Greek is *pas*, meaning all, any, or every.

The in Greek is a specific article *ho* (masculine), *hay* (feminine), and *to* (neuter); and it's *to* here.

Man in Greek is *aner*, meaning male, adult male, husband or betrothed. And **men** is *anthropos* from where we get "anthropology" (study of mankind).

Woman in Greek is *gune* meaning a woman, specifically a wife. Throughout Ephesians 5, Paul uses *aner* for "husband" and *gune* for "wife".

Power in Greek is *exousia* meaning authority, permission, liberty, and power of choice. It's possibly from the word *exesti*, meaning the right to be out in public.

Angels in Greek is *aggelos* literally meaning sent to bring tidings; translated as angels or messengers.

First notice that this passage begins and ends by saying it is a tradition and a "custom" (like releasing a prisoner at Passover). We no longer live in the first century under rule of Romans and the Jewish Sanhedrin, and the churches no longer abide by this custom. But if messengers from out of town were less likely to rape women who wore wedding rings or head scarves, it might become a measure of self-protection.

The Corinthians were following Paul's instructions regarding head coverings for women, but not for men keeping their hair short and uncovered when praying. Paul's first point is the order of responsibility and authority, termed "headship": Father God, Christ, husband, wife. In the Jewish society a husband had authority and responsibility for his wife, and a father had authority and responsibility for his unmarried daughters (I Cor. 7). Paul further instructed them as to why his instructions were good: a wife obeys her husband, a husband obeys Christ, and Christ obeyed His Father. Also headship of the husband is recognized because of the order of creation between equals (male and female) who are interdependent. The two questions were not rhetorical, but Paul allowed the Corinthians to ultimately judge for themselves if a woman could pray in their midst without a head covering and if men with long hair would be accepted. But wives wearing a head-covering was a custom, not a commandment of God. Paul provided the biblical precedent of a husband's headship to support the custom. So in that culture to show honor to your authority while praying and prophesying in church men would not place anything on their heads or grow their hair long, and women would place something on their heads and leave their hair long.

In the passage above, both men and women could pray and prophesy in the church.

> **Pray** in Greek is *proseuchomai*, meaning to pray toward.
> **Prophesy** in Greek is *propheteuo*, meaning to speak under inspiration, to foretell events, or to exercise the prophetic office.

But in order to keep with tradition, men were to pray/prophesy with their heads uncovered, and women were to pray/prophesy with their heads covered. Once I prophesied wearing a Santa's hat (my husband was wearing one also). I wanted to be a godly wife and show proper respect to my husband. If that took wearing a hat on Sundays, that's what I did. God sees our hearts as we seek to please Him. After I understood a hair covering was a tradition and not God's command, I ceased wearing them.

An excellent resource for this study is "Woman: God's Plan, not Man's Tradition" by Joanne Krupp.

Submit yourself to your husband because it represents the Bride submitting to Christ.

> **Submitting** yourselves one to another in the fear of God. Wives, **submit** yourselves to your own husbands, as to the Lord. <u>For the husband is the **head** of the wife, even as Christ is the head of the church</u>: and he is the savior of the body. Therefore as the church is **subject**

> to Christ, so let the wives be to their own husbands in
> every thing. (Ephesians 5:21-24)

Submitting/submit/subject is *hupotasso* in Greek, literally
meaning under assignment or arranged beneath; to be
subordinate, to yield to someone's admonition or advice.
Head is *kephale* in Greek meaning head; from the verb to
kapto meaning seize or to hold onto.

Other men will be drawn by your submission to your husband, so
you need to make it clear to other men that only your husband
deserves and receives your complete submission; and if they don't
back off immediately you will tell your husband. Your submission
to your husband is special. The general submitting to one another
is based upon areas of ministry in your church. If you are the
children's pastor, Sunday school teachers submit to you, and you
submit to the senior pastor.

> Wives, **submit** yourselves to your own husbands, as it
> is **fit** in the Lord. Husbands, love your wives, and be
> not **bitter** against them. (Colossians 3:18-19)

Submit is *hupotasso* in Greek, literally meaning under
obedience to, or orderly as arranged.
Fit is *aneko* in Greek, literally meaning to be present in the
midst; or to be proper.
Bitter is *pikraineo* in Greek meaning to be harsh, to exasperate,
to grieve, to sicken, or to irritate.

To submit to your husband is to acknowledge God's proper
arrangement of headship in the family. It does not guarantee that
your husband's final decisions will work out well. But it does
mean your husband will feel supported by you as the decision is
carried out, and that you will deal with any repercussions together
in love instead of in animosity. When a man feels his position as
head of the family is being threatened by his wife, he might
become "bitter" against her; and Paul understands and commands
the husband not to become harsh, but to pour out more love on his
wife which will help her to respect and honor him.

Some men haven't gotten that message. Just because God has arranged your husband as the head of the family does not give him the right to treat you badly. He is supposed to love you as his own body and sacrifice for you, not make you sacrifice for him.

If your husband is not a Christian, but is amenable to remain married, then demonstrate the love of Christ to him by submitting to him. A husband who feels respected is apt to show more love toward his wife and children.

> And the woman which has an husband that believes not, and if he be pleased to dwell with her, let her not leave him. For the unbelieving husband is sanctified by the wife, and the unbelieving wife is sanctified by the husband: else were your children unclean; but now are they holy. But if the unbelieving depart, let him depart. A brother or a sister is not under bondage in such cases: but God has called us to peace. For what know you, O wife, whether you shall save your husband? or how know you, O man, whether you shall save your wife? (I Cor. 7:13-16)

This Scripture provides one of the allowances for a Christian to divorce: abandonment. The others are adultery (Mat. 19:4-9), verbal abuse ("reviler/railer" in (I Cor. 5:11), or apostasy (I Cor. 5:11) which includes the refusal to work to support the family (I Tim. 5:8). Just because divorce is allowed in these cases, does not mean it should be pursued. Forgiveness and reconciliation are preferable. It is common sense that if you and/or your children's lives are being threatened (Malachi 2:14-16 "violence" and "treachery"), that you should immediately leave and seek protection. In the case of violence, reconciliation might not be possible.

Obey and subject yourself to your husband.

> The aged women likewise, that they be in behavior as becomes holiness, not false accusers, not given to much wine, teachers of good things; That they may teach the young women to be sober, to love their

husbands, to love their children, To be discreet, chaste, keepers at home, good, <u>obedient to their own husbands,</u> that the word of God be not blasphemed. (Titus 2:3-5)

Obedient is *hupotasso* in Greek, literally meaning under assignment or arranged beneath; to be subordinate, to yield to someone's admonition or advice. It is a military term for appointing troop divisions under a leader.

Note that a wife is to be obedient to her own husband, not to all men in general. There is no verse which commands husbands to obey their wives, so the order of headship is husband over the wife. In the family, the order of headship does not denote those with the better abilities but those placed in positions of authority. Military ranks are about the order of command so that objectives can be obtained. Our objective is to exemplify Christ in our marriage and family. Our heavenly Father is the Head of His spiritual Oneness, and He made it very clear that the husband/father is the head of his home. So wives, accept your position in the family unit, and give your husband the love and respect God commands you to give him, especially when you think you know better.

Likewise, you wives, be in **subjection** to your own husbands; that, if any obey not the word, they also may without the word be won by the **conversation** of the wives; While they behold your **chaste** conversation coupled with fear. . . . Even as Sara obeyed Abraham, calling him **lord**: whose daughters you are, as long as you **do well**, and are not **afraid** with any **amazement**. Likewise, you husbands, dwell with them according to knowledge, giving **honor** to the wife, as to the **weaker** vessel, and as being heirs together of the grace of life; that your prayers be not **hindered**. (I Peter 3:1-2, 6-7)

Subjection is *hupotasso* in Greek, literally meaning under obedience to, or orderly as arranged. It is a military term for appointing troop divisions under a leader.
Conversation is *anastrophe* in Greek, literally means turn one's self about; a repentant or converted life.

Chaste is *hagnos* in Greek, meaning pure and innocent.
Lord is *kurios* in Greek, meaning the one with authority to make final decisions.
Well-doer is *agathopoieo* in Greek, meaning to benefit others as a favor or duty.
Afraid is *phobeo* in Greek meaning fear or alarmed here, as opposed to reverent.
Amazement is *ptoesis* in Greek, from the root meaning to fall or fail; so falling, failure, or sudden terror.
Honor is *time* in Greek meaning price, value, precious, dignity, and esteem.
Weaker is *asthenes* in Greek meaning less strength.
Hindered is *ekkopto* in Greek, literally meaning cut down or cut off; so frustrated or un-answered.

After both spouses have offered pros and cons regarding a situation and prayed about it together yet can not reach agreement, a couple needs a tie-breaker. The husband will decide what he thinks would be best for the family (since he is to sacrificially love his wife and treat her as the weaker vessel, she should be able to rest in this decision). God doesn't say "if your husband loves and honors you, then submit to him;" He just commands wives to submit to their husbands and commands husbands to love their wives. Each spouse must obey the Lord's commands regardless if the other spouse does or not. But if one begins demonstrating love and respect, what goes around will come around.

The wife does not have to obey a husband's direction to commit sin or to allow herself to be abused. Husband and wife does not equate to master and slave; though a woman who has a heart of service toward her husband will do well (I Peter 3:6).

Christ will subdue all things unto His Father

Then comes the end, when he shall have **delivered up** the kingdom to God, even the Father; when he shall have put down all rule and all authority and power. For he must reign, till he has put all enemies **under** his feet. The last enemy that shall be destroyed is death. For he has put all things **under** his feet. But when he said all things are put under him, it is manifest that he

is excepted, which did put all things **under** him. And
when all things shall be **subdued** to him, then shall the
Son also himself be **subject** to him that put all things
under him, that God may be all in all.
(I Corinthians 15:24-28)

Delivered up is *paradidomi* in Greek meaning to surrender
or yield or transmit.
first **Under** is *hupo* in Greek.
second and third and fourth **Under** are *hupotasso* in Greek,
meaning under obedience.
Subdue/subject are *hupotasso* in Greek, literally meaning
under obedience to, or orderly as arranged.

After Christ's millennial reign when He has conquered all evil
authorities, He will hand over His entire kingdom to His Father
and willingly submit Himself to His Father as Head. Our Savior
isn't commanding us to do anything that He hasn't done or will do.
If we understand headship in the Trinity as a family unit, we will
understand why headship is needed in our own family units.

Let this mind be in you, which was also in Christ Jesus:
Who, being in the form of God, thought it not robbery
to be equal with God: But made himself of no
reputation, and took on him the form of a servant, and
was made in the likeness of men: And being found in
fashion as a man, he humbled himself, and became
obedient to death, even the death of the cross. Why
God also has highly exalted him, and given him a name
which is above every name: That at the name of Jesus
every knee should bow, of things in heaven, and things
in earth, and things under the earth; And that every
tongue should confess that Jesus Christ is Lord, to the
glory of God the Father. Why, my beloved, as you have
always **obeyed**, not as in my presence only, but now
much more in my absence, work out your own
salvation with fear and trembling. (Phil. 2:5-12)

Christ humbled Himself as a servant and obeyed His Father, and the Father will exalt Jesus which will bring glory to His Father: a circle of submission.

> For I have not spoken of myself; but the Father which sent me, he gave me a commandment, what I should say, and what I should speak. And I know that his commandment is life everlasting: whatever I speak therefore, even as the Father said to me, so I speak. (John 12:49-50)

The headship of the family unit is built upon firm trust and simple obedience.

> However, when he, the Spirit of truth, is come, he will guide you into all truth: for he shall not speak of himself; but whatever he shall hear, that shall he speak: and he will show you things to come. He shall glorify me: for he shall receive of mine, and shall show it to you. All things that the Father has are mine: therefore said I, that he shall take of mine, and shall show it to you. (John 16:13-15)

The Holy Spirit speaks what He hears. The Spirit receives of Christ and reveals it to us. Jesus has all that the Father has, and the Spirit will take of it and reveal it to us. Round and round the interdependence of headship goes so that God is glorified. In today's world, your loving submission to your husband stands out like a beacon pointing to the heavenly Father, Son, and Spirit.

Our American culture which emasculates men and encourages wives to be rebellious has doomed marriages. If you are struggling to submit to your husband, I recommend Dr. Debbie Cherry's book, *The Strong-Willed Wife*. She emphasizes oneness through submission.

Silence and Teaching regarding Women

This chapter is divided into the following four parts:

1. Men and women prophesied and governed.

2. Women taught and preached.

3. Paul's verses on "silence" in I Corinthians 14

4. Paul's verses on "silence" and "teaching" in I Timothy 2

Men and women prophesied and governed

Old Testament Examples

> And Miriam the prophetess, the sister of Aaron, took a tambourine in her hand; and all the women went out after her with tambourines and with dances. And Miriam answered them, Sing you to the LORD, for he has triumphed gloriously; the horse and his rider has he thrown into the sea. (Exodus 15:20-21)

> **Prophetess** is *nebiyah* in Hebrew, the feminine form of *nabiy*, meaning a prophetess.

Huldah was a prophetess (I Kings 22:14), and so was Noadiah (Nehemiah 6:14). Isaiah went to a prophetess (Isaiah 8:3); and Jesus' parents spoke with Anna, the prophetess (Luke 2:36). There were also kings and queens of Israel and Judah (II Chron. 15:16; I Kings 16:31). And Esther became queen of Persia, able to stop the slaughter of her people.

> And Deborah, a prophetess, the wife of Lapidoth, she **judged** Israel at that time. And she dwelled under the palm tree of Deborah between Ramah and Bethel in mount Ephraim: and the children of Israel came up to her for judgment. (Judges 4:4-5)

> **Judged** is *shaphat* in Hebrew meaning judge, rule, litigate, and govern.

Deborah was married, yet God did not call her husband to judge the people, but her. Barak wouldn't attack their enemies unless Deborah was with him, so God gave the victory over their enemies to a woman named Jael (Judges 4).

New Testament Examples

There were 120 male and female disciples who prayed in the upper room and then were filled with the Holy Spirit and spoke in other tongues on Pentecost. Peter stood up and addressed the Jews from every nation, saying,

> But this is that which was spoken by the prophet Joel;
> And it shall come to pass in the last days, said God, I
> will pour out of my Spirit on all flesh: and your sons
> and your daughters shall prophesy, and your young
> men shall see visions, and your old men shall dream
> dreams: And on my servants and on my handmaidens I
> will pour out in those days of my Spirit; and they shall
> prophesy: (Acts 2:16-18)

The Jews of that day did not teach the Torah to women and did not allow them to speak in synagogue. But Elohim poured out His Spirit on males and females, enabling them all to prophesy. God's Word triumphed over man's traditions. Paul interacted with men and women who prophesied.

> And the next day we that were of Paul's company
> departed, and came to Caesarea: and we entered into
> the house of Philip the evangelist, which was one of
> the seven; and stayed with him. And the same man had
> four daughters, virgins, which did prophesy. And as we
> tarried there many days, there came down from Judaea
> a certain prophet, named Agabus. (Acts 21:8-10)

Women taught and preached

> The words of king Lemuel, the prophecy that his
> mother **taught** him. (Proverbs 31:1)

Taught is *yasar* in Hebrew meaning reprove, correct, instruct, and chasten.

> And a certain Jew named Apollos, born at Alexandria,
> an eloquent man, and mighty in the scriptures, came to
> Ephesus. This man was instructed in the way of the

> Lord; and being fervent in the spirit, he spoke and
> taught diligently the things of the Lord, knowing only
> the baptism of John. And he began to speak boldly in
> the synagogue: whom when <u>Aquila and Priscilla</u> had
> heard, they took him to them, and expounded to him
> the way of God more perfectly. (Acts 18:24-26)

The dominant speaker or teacher of a ministering pair is named
first (Acts 14:12-14), like Paul and Barnabas (Acts 13:43-50).
Aquila and Priscilla taught Apollos. Later, Priscilla is named first.

> Greet Priscilla and Aquila my helpers in Christ Jesus:
> Who have for my life laid down their own necks: to
> whom not only I give thanks, but also all the churches
> of the Gentiles. Likewise greet the church that is in
> their house. (Romans 16:3-5)

> O God, when you went forth before your people, when
> you did march through the wilderness; Selah: The earth
> shook, the heavens also dropped at the presence of
> God: even Sinai itself was moved at the presence of
> God, the God of Israel. You, O God, did send a
> plentiful rain, whereby you did confirm your
> inheritance, when it was weary. Your congregation has
> dwelled therein: you, O God, have prepared of your
> goodness for the poor. The Lord gave the word: <u>great
> was the company of those that published it.</u>
> (Psalm 68:7-11)

The last phrase, according to Clarke, is *hammebasseroth tsaba rab*;
"Of the female preachers there was a great host."

Paul's verses on "silence" in I Corinthians 14

Paul's letter to the church in Corinth was largely in response to a
letter sent to him regarding certain issues. Paul praised them for
keeping the custom of married women covering their heads (I Cor.
11:2), but was displeased with how they were celebrating
communion (I Cor. 11:17). Then Paul described spiritual gifts
which are given to every (male and female) member of the body of

Christ (I Cor. 12) to be exercised in love (I Cor. 13). Then Paul goes into particular practice of spiritual gifts in the church service. Paul wants them all to speak in tongues and to prophesy, but to do so in an orderly fashion.

> If any man speak in an unknown tongue, let it be by two, or at the most by three, and that by course; and let one interpret. But if there be no interpreter, let him keep **silence** in the church; and let him speak to himself, and to God. Let the prophets speak two or three, and let the other judge. If any thing be revealed to another that sits by, let the first **hold** his **peace**. <u>For you may all prophesy one by one</u>, that all may learn, and all may be comforted. (I Cor. 14:27-31)

Silence and **hold peace** are *sigao* in Greek from the root *sige* (to hush), meaning to keep silent.

Paul instructed those speaking in tongues to the church to be silent if there is no interpreter. Paul instructed the person who prophesied to the church first to be silent if God has given someone else a prophecy for the church. Since he's on the theme of when to be silent in the church, he quotes part of their letter to him:

> Let your women keep **silence** in the churches: for it is not permitted to them to speak; but [they are commanded] to be under obedience as also **said** the **law**. And if they will learn any thing, let them ask their husbands at home: for it is a shame for women to speak in the church. (I Cor. 14:34-35; words in brackets were added by translator, and are not in the Greek manuscript)

Silence is *sigao* in Greek from the root *sige* (to hush), meaning to keep silent.
Said is *lego* in Greek meaning to "lay forth", speak, or teach.
Law is *nomos* in Greek meaning "anything received by usage, a custom, a law, a command" according to Thayer.

Recall the Jewish traditions of oral law (*paradosis* in Greek for "ordinances" in I Cor. 11:2) which was written during the Babylonian exile (known as the Babylonian Talmud) that did not allow women to speak in public or to give testimony in court.

Note that this was a spoken "law" ("said the law") and not the written word of God ("it is written"). There is no command to silence women in the Old Testament; this "law" is from the oral law of the Babylonian Talmud. After Paul quotes their letter, he responds with the following questions of exasperation:

> What? came the **word of God** out from you? or came it to you only? If any man think himself to be a prophet, or spiritual, let him acknowledge that the things that I write to you are the **commandments** of the Lord. But if any man be ignorant, let him be ignorant. Why, brothers, covet to prophesy, and forbid not to speak with tongues. Let all things be done decently and in order. (I Cor. 14:36-40)
>
> **Word of God** is *logos theos* in Greek.
> **Commandments** is *entole* in Greek meaning an authoritative precept.

Paul countered the oral Talmud with the written word of God. If a man chooses to reject the knowledge of God's Word, let him be a fool ("ignorant"). But the brothers in Christ should not forbid anyone, male or female, from speaking in tongues and prophesying; but to see it is done in the order Paul gave. Paul continued to treat women as "co-heirs in Christ," often mentioning women as fellow laborers with him in his ministry. This interpretation of I Corinthians 14 best fits the way Paul related to women.

Paul's verses on "silence" and "teaching" in I Timothy 2

> Whereunto I am ordained a preacher, and an apostle, (I speak the truth in Christ, and lie not;) a teacher of the Gentiles in faith and verity. I will therefore that men

pray every where, lifting up holy hands, without wrath
and doubting. In like manner also, that women adorn
themselves in modest apparel, with modesty and
sobriety; not with braided hair, or gold, or pearls, or
costly array; But (which becomes women professing
godliness) with good works. Let the woman learn in
silence with all **subjection**. But I suffer not a **woman**
to **teach**, nor to **usurp authority over** the man, but to
be in **silence**. For Adam was first formed, then Eve.
And Adam was not deceived, but the woman being
deceived was in the transgression. Notwithstanding she
shall be saved in childbearing, if they continue in faith
and charity and holiness with sobriety. (I Tim. 2:7-15)

Silence is *hesuchia* in Greek (the root means to keep one's seat),
meaning stillness, quietness and not disruptive.
Subjection is *huptage* (noun form of *hupotasso*), meaning
obedience and submission.
Woman is *gune* in Greek meaning woman or wife.
Teach is *didasko* in Greek meaning discourse, instruction, and
instill doctrine.
Usurp authority over is *authentio* in Greek meaning "one who
with his own hands kills another or himself" according to
Thayer. This is the only time this word is used in the New
Testament, and it was poorly translated.

Paul was writing to Timothy, a church leader at Ephesus where the
temple of Diana was. At that pagan temple female prostitutes were
the leaders who taught that Eve was created first and that women
had higher knowledge since Eve ate the forbidden fruit first.
Diana's priestesses would also dress seductively and seduce men
only to make them a human sacrifice (Proverbs 5:3-5), or to act out
sacrificing them after fornicating with them, and then sacrificing
the resultant child. Paul was dealing with Diana's priestesses
entering the church without changing their ways. Paul makes it
clear they must change and exhibit faith and holiness by wearing
modest clothing, stop seducing and "sacrificing" men or teaching
them false doctrine, and start rearing the children they bear instead
of killing them.

So after reconsidering Paul's teaching, it is clear that Paul came against the Jewish Talmudic doctrine of women being silent in public.

> But the manifestation of the Spirit is given to **every man** to profit with. For to one is given by the Spirit the word of wisdom; to another the word of knowledge by the same Spirit; To another faith by the same Spirit; to another the gifts of healing by the same Spirit; To another the working of miracles; to another prophecy; to another discerning of spirits; to another divers kinds of tongues; to another the interpretation of tongues: But all these works that one and the selfsame Spirit, dividing to **every man** severally as he will. For as the body is one, and has many members, and all the members of that one body, being many, are one body: so also is Christ. For by one Spirit are we all baptized into one body, whether we be Jews or Gentiles, whether we be bond or free; and have been all made to drink into one Spirit. (I Cor. 12:7-13)

Every man is *hekatasos* in Greek meaning everyone.

The spiritual gifts are for all believers; men women, and children. Women could use the speaking gifts in the church along with men if they all did so in an orderly fashion.

But sadly, even supposedly "Spirit-filled" churches rarely allow time or room for the gifts of God's Spirit. There is a dire need for male and female ministers of the gospel and for biblically ordered house churches who follow Christ's Spirit and mark and avoid those who teach false doctrine.

> I commend to you Phebe our sister, which is a servant of the church which is at Cenchrea: That you receive her in the Lord, as becomes saints, and that you assist her in whatever business she has need of you: for she has been a succorer of many, and of myself also. Greet Priscilla and Aquila my helpers in Christ Jesus: Who

have for my life laid down their own necks: to whom not only I give thanks, but also all the churches of the Gentiles. Likewise greet the church that is in their house. . . . Now I beseech you, brothers, mark them which cause divisions and offenses contrary to the doctrine which you have learned; and avoid them. For they that are such serve not our Lord Jesus Christ, but their own belly; and by good words and fair speeches deceive the hearts of the simple. (Rom. 16:1-5, 17-18)

Men will continue to try to enslave women and shut them up, but Jesus will continue to set women free and give them a platform to teach His Word.

Who in the days of his flesh, when he had offered up prayers and supplications with strong crying and tears to him that was able to save him from death, and was heard in that he feared; Though he were a Son, yet learned he obedience by the things which he suffered; And being made perfect, he became the author of eternal salvation to all them that obey him; Called of God an high priest after the order of Melchisedec. (Hebrews 5:7-10)

Strong crying in Greek is *is khoo-ros' krow-gay',* meaning *forcible outcry*: - boisterous clamour, or powerful screams.
Suffered in Greek is *pas'-kho, path'-o, pen'-tho,* meaning to *experience* a sensation or impression (usually painful): - feel, passion, suffer, vex.
Being made perfect in Greek is *tel-i-o'-o,* to *complete,* that is, (literally) *accomplish,* or (figuratively) *consummate* (in character): - consecrate, finish, fulfill, (make) perfect.

The Son of God needed to experience suffering in obeying His Father's will to be perfect and complete so as to offer us "eternal salvation". Somehow Peter, James and John slept through Jesus' loud crying and agonized screams in the Garden of Gethsemane. Jesus capillaries burst from the internal pressure, causing Him to sweat blood. He has heard our screams and has seen our tears, and He will walk through your sufferings with you.

www.ingramcontent.com/pod-product-compliance
Lightning Source LLC
Chambersburg PA
CBHW020037040426
42331CB00031B/945